The Reality of Society

Verses on life and living

Manmohan Shukla

First Published in May 2022

ISBN: 978-93-5611-127-1

Price: INR 200

BLUEROSE PUBLISHERS

www.BlueRoseONE.com

info@bluerosepublishers.com

+91 8882 898 898

To all my friends...

The angels in my life

Contents

Introduction 1

Prologue 3

Reality of Life and Society 5

Quotes which have an impact on our lives 5

Adoration is the only source to get salvation and many challenges to become a successful person!! 15

Deception teaches us many things. 52

Quotes For Motivational 61

Here explained every quote that is based on true life 61

True things on life 73

Success never goes wrong provided we should try repeatedly. 73

Respect of others and parents 85

Honour of others and guardian and value of meals

Introduction

Dear readers, I wrote this book because a lot of things are happening in our society, and I know many people are being harassed in many ways by their owners, officers, etc. As you know some people have many ideas to establish a business but they are unable to take such initiative because of reasons. Almost all the quotes are true for society and if you focus on them, then they will show the reality of society. My main purpose for writing this book is to explain everything by quotes, that's why I have shared my experience with you.

Prologue

Society is poison for a true human being because society is full of bad people who never let you become an honest person. (QT 1.1)

Without confidence, you can never be a successful person, and for that, you need to look at yourself. (QT 1.2)

A fragrant flower attracts you, similarly, an honest person shows his identity by doing deeds. (QT 1.3)

Worship is the only way to attain salvation and self-satisfaction. (QT 1.4)

The Reality of Life and Society.

Quotes which have an impact on our lives.

Never let someone judge your choice because they never went through your pain, and they never walked in your shoes. (MM 1.1)

Explanation: One should not judge someone's choice. Because only the victim knows the pain of the road. That's why no one can understand the pain better than them. Solely, the victim can turn his or her way by following the dedication.

*****

In KaliYuga, we are fighting for God because everyone wants to put their god at the top while God is one. (MM 1.2)

Explanation: In KaliYuga, I saw that, there are mainly four religions in this world: Hindu, Muslim, Sikh, and Christian. All religions say that I have come on this earth first and my religion is above all religions whereas reality is something

Don't judge people by their faces, they may be full of abilities. (MM 1.3)

Explanation: Some people are not what they seem, they have ability in some subjects which an intelligent person does not have, so check their ability before the exam.

*****

Excess fat always harms the body and it makes the whole body hollow day by day. (MM 1.4)

Explanation: Nowadays people are consuming a lot of refined oil in their food and it is harming us completely. People should avoid refined oil in their food and drink so that people can stay healthy, otherwise you will have to pay money to doctors

Love your kids before class and teach every good thing day by day, but remember overload always destroys thinking ability. (MM 1.5)

Explanation: Some parents love their children very much and they want to teach them everything. But some parents want their children to fulfil their every wish. It should not happen. Sometimes we force them to fulfil their dreams. So all such things are always becoming dangerous like the ability to forget etc. So don't put too much burden on your kids.

*****

Addiction ruins relationships, just as wrong decisions ruin future plans. (MM 1.6)

Explanation: People in this world consume alcohol every day. According to the world's population and details, the consumption of alcohol by the people by 2020 was about 6.5 billion litres, the most dangerous thing for the middle-class family and others. If we talk about India then almost all the

Cheating is a part of life because everyone wants to use it to their advantage. (MM 1.7)

Explanation: Cheating has become a part of life. You can see this in society. Many are waiting to deceive you. I am not pointing out everyone, but some people in this world want to cheat you and take over your entire property. So beware of such people, there may be some people in your family too.

*****

The state of death teaches us to take up arms, if you don't take anything, others can take your life. (MM 1.8)

Explanation: Many criminals and fraudsters are roaming

The pen has more strength than the muscles of the body, You use muscles for anything, but with a pen, you can force everyone to follow you. (MM 1.9)

Explanation: Nowadays, the gym has become a popular place to maintain your body. They balance their diet, and they work hard and pay fees to the owner so that they can stay fit, you can scare people with muscle power but there are many illiterate people, and they don't know the power of a pen. You can force everyone to follow you with a pen.

*****

It is good to read book or novel to gain knowledge and it works in adversity. (MM 1.10)

Explanation: There are 130 billion people in our country. Almost everyone is attached to books. Reading books is never

Dreams always come true but they should be seen with open eyes. (MM 1.11)

Explanation: Dreams are a gift from God, and everyone dreams in their sleep. If you see this dream at midnight then it may be fake but if you see it in the morning then according to my experience, it comes true, as you know, everyone has a dream in life and Somebody wants to accomplish it by hard work etc.

*****

Morning always brings a beautiful meaning to our lives, but it is in our hands how we make it. (MM 1. 12)

Explanation: Every morning is a natural gift. This happens according to the laws of nature. Everyone waits for

Exploitation has become a part of life because everyone wants to use it to humiliate mankind. (MM 1. 13)

Explanation: Exploitation has become a curse for mankind. Everyone wants to use it for their benefit, Exploitation is not from this time, it has been going on for very long decades, which is very difficult to explain. You have been a victim day by day and will continue to be.

*****

It is very easy to upset poor people, because they are illiterate and can not do anything against rich people etc. (MM 1. 14)

Explanation: As you know, all the rules and regulations are for the poor. It is very easy to harass poor people. I have seen

Knowledge comes from good books, not books written by a bad writer. (MM 1.15)

Explanation: Knowledge is essential for mankind. Without it, we can survive but not properly. For good life and a bright future we have to take the knowledge through school, college etc. provided it is from good places. As you know many people are playing with your history and they all write fake stories. Such people always want to defame our civilizations so you have to find out who is a good writer or a bad one. So always choose good people for good guidance.

*****

Birds do not have GPS or compass but even after that they reach home everyday, they know the direction, that is, we should know nature. (MM 1.16)

There is no difference between boys and girls, but the point of view should be different. (MM 1. 17)

Explanation: In this KaliYuga, some hypocritical people create differences between girls and boys. I am not talking about all that but there are only a few people who are illiterate and they differentiate between girls and boys. Some people consider girls as goddesses and have great respect for them. But some hypocrites get her killed by having abortions etc.

*****

The medicine does not work in a situation where there is no confidence. (MM 1.18)

Explanation: Almost everyone is suffering from diseases due to their lifestyle. Our lifestyle affects us and it also brings many types of infections. If we want to be healthy then we

Adoration is the only source to get salvation and many challenges to become a successful person!!

Everything is dependent on time, without it, nothing is impossible. If someone did not follow the time, he did not succeed. (MM 2. 1)

Explanation: Time plays an important role in our life. I have seen in my midst that only a few people are punctual. And some people do not know the value of time, so such a person is always behind in society, without this, you cannot achieve your goal in future and birth and death are also dependent on time. So, in my view, we are incapable of doing anything before that, and that should always be a priority. You should always be punctual.

*****

Everyone wants to be honest but greed takes over. (MM 2.2)

Explanation: Honesty is never seen on the face, it has to express itself. But I have seen that there is a dearth of honest people in all departments, and still dishonest people always

Inflation defies the rules of the government, similarly, the failure of the guardian destroys the unity of the children. (MM 2.3)

Explanation: Inflation affects all aspects of the economy, from consumer spending, trade, investment and employment rates to government progress, tax policies and interest rates. Inflation can reduce the value of investment returns. Similarly, parents play an important role in maintaining the unity of the family and they should give equal education to their children. So that they are not deprived of education, but some parents do not pay attention to the education of their children, as a result, such parents are unable to stand their generation.

*****

The name has its own meaning because a man's

You can meet your expenses with your salary, but not your desire, for this, you have to choose your business. (MM 2.5)

Explanation: There are 130 billion people in India and almost all people like government and private work so that they do not have to suffer. you can fulfil your needs by the job but not desires, for that you have to do business if you want to be succeed in future.

*****

Business teaches you to control yourself, whereas a government job teaches you to be angry because it depends on money. (MM 2.6)

Explanation: Why am I giving importance to business? This is because there is a lot of hope for fulfilling your dream in business. As you know there is a lot of money where you

A wild animal cannot improve its nature, because they know that we are not made for human love. (MM 2.7)

Explanation: A wild animal searches for its food, shelter, water and all its other needs. However, some foolish people keep them as pets and keep them in the house, which is fraught with risk. Sometimes wild animals attack their master when they are hungry. We have many examples among us. So, in my view, we should not keep them at home.

*****

The ego destroys itself, while love brings about the strongest bond between the family. (MM 2.8)

Explanation: ego is making mankind hollow. Ego has had a bad effect on mankind while love plays an important role

A straight road is always good to walk, just like a crooked road is always dangerous to drive, life is too short, take it easy. (MM 2.9)

Explanation: As you know today the world is full of challenges. People walk fast on a crooked road and get entangled in it. As everyone knows that life is very short but people are confused on that too. In such a situation, it becomes difficult to drive on a crooked road. Similarly, devious decisions can also be avoided.

*****

Just as an angry man cannot give up his nature and an arrogant man cannot leave his ego, similarly a woman cannot change her nature, no matter what the situation. (MM 2.10)

Explanation: She has the same human nature as a man, but I have seen almost everywhere, that when some women are in a good position, they talk rudely with people. This is my personal experience, I am not against them, I have a lot of

It is easy to upset the bride but not the daughters and one day it will be repeated by the daughters. (MM 2.11)

Explanation: Dowry has become the biggest enemy for the poor family in India. Because of this, they are not able to get married in society and in-laws harass them for dowry. If some people are unable to give dowry then they kill the bride in many ways. In my view, dowry should be banned from society forever.

*****

Cutting a tree will destroy nature, similarly, a dispute can destroy your strength. (MM 2.12)

Explanation: As we know that trees play an important role in saving our nature but due to development local bodies are

There is no disease like hunger, you can fight with any disease, but you cannot fight hunger, this problem will force you to eat anything. (MM 2.13)

Explanation: India is an agricultural country, and many people depend on their agricultural land. Even after that, some people fall asleep without eating food. such people always search the food to fulfil their hunger, you can survive in sickness, not hunger and it forces you to eat anything. That's why I am saying don't waste food because wasted food can fill a hungry stomach.

*****

The one who progresses is respected, in the same way, as the Sun is worshipped in Hinduism. (MM 2.14)

Explanation: In Hindu culture, people worship the sun in the morning in many ways. Similarly, everyone likes those

Those who create their drama, they are the characters of their deeds. (MM 2.15)

Explanation: People's work depends on their karma, but hard work is associated with success. People probably blame their fate because they have forgotten their duty.

*****

Life is like a wheel, just as a wheel is important to a vehicle, just as good behaviour is important to a human being. (MM 2.16)

Explanation: Life comes with many obstacles and is full of challenges, even then people face them and choose their path towards success, similarly, the vehicle is naked without wheels and human is incomplete without good behaviour.

Never take your girl from house to house. No one knows when whose nature will change. (MM 2.17)

Explanation We cannot guarantee anyone's behaviour. In my view, you can free your daughters but within limits. More importantly, people should take care of their daughters because many bad people are roaming around in society who stare at girls.

*****

Imaginary property will never work for your generation, if your next responsible is not educated. (MM 2.18)

Explanation: I have seen in society that some people are busy increasing their wealth by not paying attention to their children's education so that the next generation can live

Breathing is like a keypad, no one knows, when it will stop on its own. (MM 2.19)

Explanation: Human is like a candle, no one knows when it will melt. Nowadays there is a lot of infection among us and almost everyone is suffering from infection. We have completely changed our lifestyle by eating fast food etc. Therefore we are in big trouble and we make rounds to the hospital.

*****

Always avoid such people who call you right in everything, because such people will never save you when you need it. (MM 2.20)

Explanation: You will find many people in the society who will justify your mistake but you should avoid such people

Just as dense trees shelter during the journey, similarly, an obedient son gives shelter to his parents in old age. (MM 2.21)

Explanation: Trees play an important role on this earth. Every living being needs shelter because it gives you relief when you are at rest. You need to save all the things of nature for your future generation, otherwise, you will be in big trouble. Similarly, a wise child provides shelter to his parents in old age. so that they do not feel alone. Both aspects are important in their place.

*****

There is nothing to be gained by being jealous, people waste their precious time on the fate of others instead of making their luck. (MM 2. 22)

Explanation: Everything can be achieved by working hard.

The love of God for a true devotee is as deep, as the love of a mother for a child. (MM 2.23)

Explanation: It has been seen in ancient times that some noble people have had philosophy of God according to their karma and God never leaves the side of those who worship him with true heart. In the same way, a mother also loves her children and never wants to see them in trouble. But we also have a responsibility to support them in their old age.

*****

Earnings from domestic interest are never useful, just as, the body is never used after burning. (MM 2.24)

Explanation: In ancient times there used to be moneylenders whose job was to give money to people for domestic interest, but some people are using it arbitrarily. People take advantage of their problems and arbitrarily give money to people at interest which is very difficult to repay.

Illiteracy brings darkness to our life, similarly, literacy brings light to our life. (MM 2.25)

Explanation: It is seen in our society that some people do not give importance to literacy and do not take it seriously. Maybe they don't know the reality of it. Those who do not have knowledge are always dumb. Live in the society like a deaf and the one who has knowledge gets a good place in the society.

*****

Never cry in front of anyone other than your parents, because by doing so you look weak. (MM 2.26)

Explanation: As you know that crying is a natural action for a living being. People cry in two situations, first when he

The weak man always hides his mistake, and he never tries to support the truth, such people always remain cowards. (MM2.27)

Explanation: There are two types of people among us, the timid and the fearless. However, almost everyone supports the wrong things for their benefit. Some people dare to stand up against the wrong things and others never support the truth. Honest people die alive, so always support truth in your life.

*****

Love marriage flows like a water tank, no one knows when it will fall. (MM 2.28)

Explanation: Love marriage is such a marriage in which there is neither trust nor familyism. It can be from any caste. I have seen that people often cheat in a love marriage. Some

People want to end humanity by discrimination, while humanity creates heaven around us. (MM 2.29)

Explanation: By not discriminating, we can make mankind more beautiful. But in the society you will find such people who will defame the human race and will keep humiliating them by discriminating against each other.

*****

We practice handwriting to improve our writing, in the same way, hardworking never goes in vain to become a successful person. (MM 2.30)

Explanation: Everything matters in life, illiterate life is like a tailless dog, we practice handwriting and we encourage others to do the same. Similarly, hard work never goes in vain, it brings shine to our life. That's why we should not

When we are helpless and we do not see any help in front, then we should surrender otherwise war will destroy everything. strengthen yourself. (MM 2.31)

Explanation: When we have a threat from the front and we feel that we cannot face that danger, then we should surrender. Otherwise, we will destroy our people along with us. To win any battle, we have to make ourselves strong, only then we can face someone.

*****

Dowry is the worst thing in this world because it acts as a kind of infection. (MM 2.32)

Explanation. Dowry has become a curse in India. Some people even sell their land and property to give dowry which works to humiliate mankind.

Nature and time play a vital role in developing things, we are just one direction. (MM 2.33)

Explanation: Almost everyone thinks that I am behind things. But I would like to clarify that nature keeps on changing with time. As I have seen in this society, many people say that they have raised their children etc. But nothing like that, we just did our duty and nothing else. We are just one direction.

*****

Eating curd is like poison at night, good during the day, milk is good at night and bad during the day. (MM 2.34)

Explanation: Everyone knows that milk and curd are loaded with their nutrients, but using it incorrectly can ruin your acidity. So you choose it at the right time so that you

We born from the womb but completes the journey in the grave, so never be arrogant. (MM 2.35)

Explanation: Some people in society use their egos to hurt the humanity of others. By doing humanity we can make mankind beautiful.

*****

Never forget a friend's favour and always help him in adversity because mutual understanding brings strength between you. (MM 2.36)

Explanation: There are good and bad friends in society, but you should not forget the support of such a friend throughout your life, who supported you in your calamity. If possible, you should support him even in his calamity, only

Eating early dinner, sleeping for 6 hours and getting up in Brahma Muhurta, all these things change our life and keep us healthy. (MM 2.37)

Explanation: As per the advice of doctors we should eat dinner early as it takes around 12 hours to get digested completely so that our internal organs can work smoothly. If you pay attention to this then it will definitely change your life. We should take food according to the time. And in the same way getting up in Brahma Muhurta and taking bath and worshiping before sunrise changes our life. Try it out once.

*****

Adoration protects you from stress because it has a lot of power itself so never try to get away from it. (MM 2.38)

Satisfaction is a great weapon of life because if you have it then you can avoid taking debt. (MM 2.39)

Explanation: Satisfaction is a multipurpose medicine, it works in every situation. If you have contentment then you can handle everything throughout your life otherwise you will be troubled.

*****

Debt takes us to hell, if possible it should be avoided. (MM 2.40)

Explanation: Nowadays, we keep a lot of ambitions and expenses to fulfil all our dreams. We take loans from banks or from anywhere else. It affects our normal life. If some people are not able to repay the loan then they are compelled

Human are born in every houses, but humanity is born in some houses. (MM 2.41)

Explanation: You are human and it is your responsibility to show your humanity to nature and others. But it is getting lost in society, people have forgotten their duty and are engaged in harassing others. No one wants to help others, it seems that humanity has left us. You need to grab it because without humanity human beings have nothing but bad thoughts.

*****

Those who eat meat and drink wine and those who remain illiterate are all wicked in human disguise and the earth bears their burden. (MM 2.42)

Explanation: It has been seen that some people kill innocent animals to satisfy their hunger which is against

Those who do not have confidence work like servants and those who have confidence work like businessmen. (MM 2.43)

Explanation: In India, a lot of people prefer job because they don't want to do hard work. Such people are always dependent on their salary and push their life. Such people cannot fulfil their dream. People who are dependent on their monthly wages don't become a millionaire. For fulfilling dreams you have to establish your business, then your dream can come true and you will be able to accomplish your wishes. For example, have you seen Gujarati's in the job? Probably not because they believe in business, not in the job.

*****

Many challenges to become a successful person

Don't close the book when bad things happen in your life. just turn the page and begin your life. (MM 3.1)

Explanation: Have you seen in the society that some people get frustrated after seeing bad times and lower their morale And some take wrong steps. Bad times don't last forever, one day it ends, so don't get upset after seeing bad times and just keep climbing to make your life better and better. you will see the goal is ahead.

*****

The layout of the sleepers defines the living conditions of the house, similarly, much makeup defines the character of the teacher. (MM 3.2)

Explanation: living conditions of the house matter in society, and from this, you can get an idea of what the

Never care about those who criticize because such people always come under the category of a fool. (MM 3.3)

Explanation: You will also find such people in the society who will criticize you after seeing your progress and keep demoralizing you with critical things, then you should not pay attention to such people and move towards your goal because such people will always be in that category of stupid, Who never let anyone grow.

*****

A woman may be helpless in domestic violence, because she cares about the family but the more oppressed can teach us a good lesson. (MM 3.4)

Explanation: It is seen in society that domestic violence is

The calmness of the spouse is a good thing during the dispute, it reduces the conflicts in the relationship. (MM 3.5)

Explanation: During domestic violence, it has been seen that some women use derogatory words and keep insulting others which should not be there. They should maintain peace during domestic violence because with peace you can achieve everything and also remove your violence. Therefore it is necessary to maintain peace.

*****

Always maintain your decision with morale, because only with morale you can achieve everything. (MM 3.6)

Explanation: It is seen that some people do not work with

It is very easy to become a hermit, but it is very difficult to maintain it, Similarly, it is easy to become a soldier, but very difficult to complete its test. (MM 3.7)

Explanation: There is no practice required to become a sanyasi and no formal registration is required, It can be made hermit only by his determination, When a sanyasi goes to his monastery, the sanyasi has to undergo a rigorous test. Even after becoming a sanyasi, first of all he has to take alms from his home which is very difficult but a sanyasi does so. In the same way it is easy to become a soldier, but to get his test and pass the test is as difficult as becoming a sanyasi.

*****

Marriage doesn't complete without three means, until God is not the centre of it. (MM 3.8).

Be respectful to other people, it might not mean anything to you, but it could mean everything to them. (MM 3.9)

Explanation: Behaviour is an important thing in our life. Without it, there can be no welfare of human life. Respect shows your sensitivity towards others. Therefore elders should be respected and elders' blessings should also be taken.

*****

Life is like a stock market no one knows when time will prevail. (MM 3.10)

Explanation: As we know that there is no guarantee of life because we are getting affected by chemicals etc. day by day. That's why I say that we should boycott such a thing

The teacher is never ordinary and the teacher is not successful until his student gets a good education. (MM 3.11)

Explanation: Education is incomplete without a teacher. Teacher plays an important role in life and they give everything to their students. They inspire others to achieve their goals. More importantly, never underestimate any teacher because they have good knowledge which you don't have. But the teacher should see all the students and identify such students who are weak in reading and work hard on them and make them equal to all.

*****

No matter what my age is, I will always need my parents. (MM 3.12)

Lust never sees a relationship. It just satisfies its hunger. (MM 3.13)

Explanation: There is no such disease as lust. It never sees the relationship, just wants to satisfy its hunger. So always be careful with such things. If you think something is about to happen then run away and defend yourself in front of the local bodies.

*****

Hard work never goes in vain, sleep gets worse and those who focus on their work, get success. (MM 3.14)

Explanation: There are many ups and downs in our destiny during the struggle but it does not mean that we should give up. We have to fight with such things so that we can survive the calamity. So never give up because those

Man can imitate everything, but he cannot imitate the fate of others. (MM 3.15)

Explanation: It is in our habit to copy. People copy the wrong things quickly, but they never copy the right things. Almost everyone can copy anything from certain people, be it good or bad. But they cannot copy the fate of others. They can achieve it only by hard work. If you want to make your future bright, then you have to think differently and find a way where you can achieve your dream.

*****

Just as a thread plays an important role in making the fabric strong, in the same way, trust is needed to make a relationship strong. (MM 3.16)

Explanation: As you know that thread plays an important role in making the fabric strong. Clothes cannot be woven

Mother is a form of God, we need to take care of her because the mother is with you in adversity, and the rest of the relationship rarely takes care of you. (MM 3.17)

Explanation: Mother cares for us because we are her children, and it is our responsibility to take care of her in times of adversity. But some foolish people leave their parents in old age. Please do not do this as she is a form of the God found in KaliYuga. Always respect and love them, they are priceless gifts to us.

*****

A flower is known by its fragrance, man by character, a teacher by his ability, a master by his knowledge and skill and authorities by his psychology. (MM 3.18)

Explanation: If a flower does not give off its fragrance, it has no meaning. Such a flower is always useless and it never

Never change your originality for the sake of others, because no one can play your role better than you. (MM 3.19)

Explanation: In society, I have seen that some people hide their identity because of others. There are so many youngsters in this line and they never show their talent. Such people are not able to choose their life because of their shy nature. Never be shy, go out. May your dream will take you further.

*****

Everyone runs after money, some people get it because they focus on their work. (MM 3.20)

Explanation: Money plays an important role in our life. Life is very difficult without it because money fulfils our

If you don't like where you are, move You are not a permanent. (MM 3.21)

Explanation: Some people give up after seeing their bad times and some people live in that condition, such people should move towards a success story where there are many goals.

*****

A drunk man may be clean in the heart but not trustworthy because such a man can deceive you into calamity or even leak your privacy. (MM 3.22).

Explanation: As you know that almost people adopt alcohol in their lifestyle and such people cannot live without it. I have seen in my life that such people may be pure in heart, but they cannot be trusted. Such people are always

Iron is strengthened by its respective chemical, in the same way, that children are strengthened by their parents. (MM 3.23)

Explanation: In the Morden region, iron is the most important of all metals, as it is important to prepare different types of steel, which are used in a wide variety of applications. Steel is used to make paper clips. Similarly, children should be strong in society as they need the suggestions of their parents in the face of adversity. Parents boost their morale and never let them fall.

*****

Blessed be the house where the family is happy, the children are courteous, the wife is dear and the girls speak deliciously and where Shiva is worshipped. (MM 3.24)

Deception teaches us many things.

Everyone works hard but very few people get the goal because luck is not the same, we have to achieve it by concentration. (MM 4.1)

Explanation: Every person has a dream and each person does his work to achieve the goal. But only a few people get this gift. If you want to make your future bright then you have to work and concentrate on yourself.

*****

You find a happy life, you make it. (MM 4.2)

Explanation: Everyone has a dream and everyone does their work to achieve the goal. But only a few people get this gift. If you want to make your future bright then you have to find your way.

There is no profit in stealing money. It is possible that the one for whom you are saving your money may spend your stolen money on useless things. (MM 4.3)

Explanation: There is no profit in stealing money. The one for whom you are saving your money may spend your stolen money on useless things.

*****

Every lesson gives a lesson and every lesson changes a person. (MM 4.4)

Explanation: Pain is a part of life, sometimes it comes from relatives and sometimes it gets children and wives etc. which cannot be shown. Such a lesson always hurts and changes a person.

Time should be used in good works, never on such things where there is no benefit. (MM 4.5)

Explanation: Some people waste their time on someone who behaves badly and they never understand their intentions. And such a person does not get anything. Never spend your precious time in such things where there is no scope. The way is in your hands.

*****

Like pen is useless without ink, a body without eyes, women without men, the court without a judge, married life without children, children without parents, a country without PM and God without devotees, all these matters for mankind. (MM 4.6)

Confidence takes us to the top provided, we don't get discouraged. (MM 4.7)

Explanation: Confidence keeps us fresh and it motivates us to move forward and execute tasks. For that many people attend motivational speeches and seminars. But no one can take you forward until you know yourself. So, identify yourself first as it is a good way to gain confidence.

*****

Sleep is necessary to remember everything, otherwise there will be upheaval in daily life. (MM 4.8)

Explanation: As you know that sleep plays an important role in our life but some people sleep till late which is not good for human beings. According to the advice of doctors, 6 or 8 hours is enough to remember everything. According to my experience if we sleep 6 or 8 hours and wake up before

Instead of fulfilling every wish of your children, give them knowledge because desires do not end and knowledge gives you a good place in society. (MM 4.9)

Explanation: Children should be knowledgeable so that they can get a good place in society, some parents fulfill their every wish and some children take advantage of it and force them to fulfill their every wish. Sometimes it is dangerous for the parents. Parents should never fulfill their wishes and demands, they should give better education so that they can fulfill every dream.

*****

DNA never leaves its effect, it remains for the next generation. (MM 4.10)

Explanation: DNA contains the instructions necessary for

Cool-looking people always keep things inside, while happy people always look happy. (MM 4.11)

Explanation: There are two types of people in our society. One who looks happy with the face and one who looks calm with the face. Silent looking man will always keep your words in his heart and will strategize against you when needed and happy looking man will always help you in adversity and will never harm you.

*****

Just as widows are being exploited, similarly, uneducated people are being exploited by some rich people. (MM 4. 12)

Explanation: I saw that widows are being exploited by some evil people in our society because some people in our society want to fulfil their lust. That's why such people stare

Education matters in job, education is not necessary to grow your business, only dedication makes your wealth better. (MM 4. 13)

Explanation: As you know that education gives us a better place in the society and without it we are like a blind person. But it is not mandatory in business because only dedication and focus can take your business forward.

*****

A woman's nature is like a spark, which is difficult to understand, even God believes, that man can melt but a woman cannot be. (MM 4.14)

Explanation: The woman is considered a form of Goddess. I have seen this in society, the nature of women is like a spark. No one knows when she will change herself. Women are behind the

Quotes For Motivational

Here explained every quote that is based on true life

In the absence of rainwater, the pond automatically absorbs the accumulated water, in the same way, all the savings of the one who spends more get wasted. (MM 5.1)

Explanation: According to sources, rainwater is more important for the pond. Without this, the pond automatically absorbs the accumulated water and it is a good way to store rainwater so that we can get water from the pond easily. Rainwater is useful for many purposes for us. Similarly, the person who spends more loses his entire savings in just a few months. If he never controls his expenses, it will take him no time to become poor. I think people should control their expenses.

*****

The clap is a symbol of human happiness because only one thing comes out of the heart. (MM 5.3)

Explanation: Clap is known to improve overall heart health and blood pressure. Secondly, clapping shows your happiness in front of the artist. I think it is a good way to impress someone and it boosts the morale of the artist. Doctors also say that clapping removes a lot of stress, so clapping plays an important role in our life.

*****

Forgive those who have argued with you and sleep well, and leave them to their deeds. (MM 5.4)

Explanation: You must have seen in society that some people are always ready to argue with you, then you should ignore such people and leave them to their karma and I

Gambling, chasing girls holds us back, you have to work hard to achieve the goal. (MM 5.5)

Explanation: People face many challenges and work hard to achieve their goals, but some people are addicted to gambling and raffle. Therefore, such actions always pull us back. History is witness, if you want to achieve your goal then you have to support good people and work hard. without it, you can never be a successful person.

*****

It is easy to commit a crime but it is difficult to feel the feelings of the victim, it is easy to give a death sentence but very difficult to hang. (MM 5.6)

Explanation: Almost everyone commits crimes under someone's influence because they are not able to think and control themselves. Some people encourage them for their

The biggest deception you do to yourself is by finding employment and spending your whole life on it, It can feed you but cannot fulfil your desires. For that, you have to go to business. (MM 5.7)

Explanation: The middle-class family always talks about employment because their ancestors also depended on it. So their generation is always in search of government/private jobs. I am not against jobs but they should be of the upper class. In lower service, people cannot fulfil their will. They can only satisfy hunger, not desire.

*****

There are always two sides to every coin provided that we must understand the right things, some are quick to know the fake truth and some are waiting for the truth. (MM 5.8)

Explanation: There are two types of people in the society who support the wrong and the other who support the truth. But there

Hope is man's worst enemy, I think only a true friend helps you in trouble. (MM 5.9)

Explanation: The expectation is our weakest point and we expect a lot from others. It should not happen. People always befriend you for selfish reasons. So you must believe in yourself and be capable of yourself.

*****

Thinking should always be on top because thinking can force you to prove someone wrong. (MM 5.10)

Explanation: Thinking plays an important role in planning. It helps to define and organize. Experience, plan, learn, reflect and create. Some people have low thinking and such people are always engaged in humiliating others. So

Income should be multiple because with one income you can suffer and you can never live your normal life. (MM 5.11)

Explanation: In India, I saw people who live on one income, whereas it should be many because we have many expenses in our life so we cannot live on one income. As you know, we cannot meet our needs by salary etc. It should be divided on various grounds.

*****

If you help someone, I'm sure he'll help you one day, so don't think that the people who need help are pretending, maybe there's some truth in their problem. (MM 5.12)

Explanation Helping some people is good but sometimes it goes wrong because some people are robbers who cheat people. So beware of such people. More importantly, you

Before Kaliyuga, there was no deceit in a war that stopped after sunset, but in Kaliyuga, deceit is at the top and your enemy is ready to win the dispute by deceit. (MM 5. 13)

Explanation: Everything has changed in this era, some people will help you in trouble, otherwise everyone wants to cheat with you. Always beware of such people, in this era there are only a few people do not want to cheat with you. Otherwise, the list is so big that it's hard to describe.

*****

Never run after girls because such things divide your path, she will force you to spend money on yourself so first set your goal and earn money. (MM 5. 14)

Explanation: Nowadays it has been seen that our younger generation has lost their way because they like to work on

Target meets focus, without focus, you'll be blinded by your path, so the focus needs to be captured. (MM 5. 15)

Explanation: To achieve anything you have to focus on the goal. Only focus makes you a successful person. But I think there is another option where you should take control of yourself. Avoid extra spending and gambling otherwise, it will bother you. If you want to achieve your goal then you have to stay away from high expenses. This is the mantra that makes us successful.

*****

Society never values empty pockets, for that, you have to earn money and fame. (MM 5.16)

Explanation: as you know, society never likes those people

If you want to change the world, then go home and love your family. (MM 5.17)

Explanation: Some people believe that we are capable of changing the world by our deeds or our speeches, but this may not be possible because the world is full of bad people who are never ready to understand the right things. I don't think, anyone can change this. World, only we can spread good ideas for all to follow. and nothing else. Because the world will run accordingly.

*****

It is very easy to defeat someone, but very difficult to win someone. (MM 5.18)

Explanation: It is seen in society that some people believe in troubling the lowly people with their deeds, maybe they

The focus should be on one task and not on many. Because such a thing always becomes a wound. (MM 5.19)

Explanation: Many people in our society do not have confidence. They choose multiple tasks due to which they are unable to focus on one goal. Such people are not able to achieve the task so in my view you should choose one thing where you can focus on working on that thing.

*****

Don't enter a place where you don't have knowledge, because such things always bring you down. (MM 5.20)

Explanation: It is seen in society that some people jump into the affairs of others without knowing the truth and

Just as an accident destroys your body, so a woman of bad character destroys your married life. (MM 5.21)

Explanation: Accidents and marriage both are different but they complement each other because you know that an accident destroys your life and sometimes it finishes your whole family. Similarly, marrying a woman of bad character can at times ruin your married life. She brings unrest to the family so never marry girls who destroy your house.

*****

Sometimes leaving a family is painful, but it is all an illusion. (MM 5.22)

Explanation: Life is a tough road and more than that it is very difficult to leave the family, No one wants to leave their

True things on life

Success never goes wrong provided, we should try repeatedly.

Never underestimate yourself, because you are the only one who can do better than others. (MM 6.1)

Explanation: It has been seen in society that, some people do not know themselves and sometimes they go out of their way after seeing the struggle. probably, they don't know that no one can do better than you, provided you will have to know your confidence.

*****

If you want to earn more money, than stock up on expensive things. (MM 6.2)

Explanation: It has been seen that almost all traders stock such things which gives them good profits in future. So if you want to earn more money and become a successful person in future then you also have to think like traders and stock such

One cannot become rich by saving money. Such money is useful only in calamity, if you want to become rich then move towards business.

Explanation: As you know that nobody can become a millionaire by investing in banks, it works in adversity. if you want to become a successful person then invest in the stock, because there is a huge profit. And those who take risks, will lead the market and those who never take risks will never succeed. So try to know the market value.

*****

There are two kinds of love, one from the heart and the other from selfishness, but the other love always loses faith. (MM 6.4)

Explanation: it has been seen in society, I would like to talk about those who cheat on girls in love, some boys do it

Always try to find the talent inside you, or else, it will be hidden forever. (MM 6.5)

Explanation: Some people never try to find their talent or show it to anyone. Such people never get a perfect future, such a person is always left behind, so don't be afraid of the target, as the risk in business or another field will take you ahead.

*****

Just as termites eat the whole wood, sugar eats the whole body, therefore, everything should be within limits. (MM 6.6)

Explanation: Too much of everything is bad. So be careful before taking any initiative. If you do not take care of the tree, termites will eat the tree. Similarly, if you do not pay

If you are afraid of losing something, remember that, trees lose their leaves every year and wait for a good day, in the same way, people should wait for a good day, because pain does not last forever. (MM 6.7)

Explanation: It has been seen that some people always lower their morale by seeing the obstacles in life. While it shouldn't be, ups and downs are a part of life. it happens sometimes. Never fear these temporary ailments. A good day will surely come.

*****

You can earn more money by mixing, but you cannot earn fame. (MM 6.8)

Explanation: You can find many such people in the society who mix their product with chemicals and earn more money

Try to know the value of life, don't waste it on social media nonsense. (MM 6.9)

Explanation: Almost everyone on social media wastes their time on useless things. Some people use it to get information about many things but some people use it only for time to pass. Which gets nothing.

*****

Love is indeed blind and some people leave their parents for happiness, but perhaps such people have forgotten that one day they too will be parents. (MM 6.10)

Explanation: I have seen in society, some hypocritical people leave their parents for their wife or love because girls force them to choose between the two, and some boys do

Instead of fulfilling the wishes of the children, we should tell them the price of those things so that they can understand the value of things. (MM 6.11)

Explanation: Every parent loves their children and parents fulfil their every need but it should not be so. Because sometimes they never understand the value of things. If they struggle to get things, they will give importance to them otherwise they will not understand and they will become dependent on others so teach them to value things.

*****

Never lose your confidence by seeing the struggle, because this is the time when you recognize yourself. (MM 6.12)

Explanation: Seeing the struggle, many people lower their

Just as a plant needs water, parents need children for the future. (MM 6.13)

Explanation: As I have mentioned in many interpretations that everything matters in life. Similarly, our parents need children to run the future. But it has been seen in society that some people leave their parents for some reason and do not pay attention to them. Perhaps they do not know that parents need their children in old age so that their old age can be well.

*****

The flicker of alcohol loses the spirit of a good man, and makes you fall. (MM 6.14)

Explanation: Addiction is like poison. Those who have adopted can never become good people at heart. There is no

Melting a hard object depends on its temperature. In the same way, melting a tough person depends on his nature. (MM 6.15)

Explanation: We make every effort to melt a hard object and bring it to its temperature. Similarly, to melt a hard person depends on his nature and sometimes it fails because his nature is very rigid.

*****

As writing is incomplete without grammar, in the same way, life is incomplete without money. (MM 6.16)

Explanation: Without money, we cannot do anything and money plays an important role in human life, people are compelled to do anything because of money. Similarly,

Business can fulfil your wish. With the job, you can compromise on your needs. (MM 6.17)

Explanation: If you want to achieve anything in your life then you have to go towards business because business is the only way where you can achieve everything. And if you are dependent on salary then you are just one step away from poverty because salary cannot meet your expenses and desires.

*****

The way the leader of the country empowers the country, in the same way, the army of the country empowers the country. (MM 6.18)

Explanation: It was seen that if the leader of a country is not strong then its citizens are insecure. In the same way, if

Don't limit your talent Always try to show your talent, because one day it will take you forward. (MM 6.19)

Explanation: Some people do not want to come forward and show their talent. Perhaps they do not know that if they hide their talent, then their talent will always be hidden and they will never be able to prove themselves in front of people. That's why I request everyone that if you can think and do something different, then definitely do it, so that people can know about your ability.

*****

The relationship between books and humans should be of friendship because books always give you the knowledge and remove your loneliness. (MM 6.20)

Explanation: As you know that there is a good relationship

Hurt someone with the truth, but never make them happy with a lie. (MM 6.21)

Explanation: In society, you will find some people who will never stop someone from doing wrong, and flattering men will encourage them to do more fake work, but they will never ask them to support or stand by the truth. If you want to please them, ask them to stand by the truth. Because honesty adorns mankind.

*****

Never tell your privacy to anyone, they can take advantage of this privacy in your adverse situation. (MM 6.22)

Explanation: It is seen in society that some people tell their privacy by trusting more people, but maybe they don't know that the person you are trusting can share your privacy among the people. That's why you should never tell your

Respect of others and parents

Honour of others and guardian and value of meals, as it fulfils hunger's needs and income and investment should be multiple.

We always try to achieve achievements, but we get disappointed, it does not mean that we should give up, we should always try to achieve the goal. (MM 7.1).

Explanation: We always try to follow our destiny so that we can get something. But luck is not the same all the time to get it. We have to work hard to achieve our goals. However, even after working hard many times, we never get our goal. But we should not give up, otherwise, we will never be able to make our future bright. So always try to grab your work and dreams.

*****

The beauty of morning comes from the whispers of birds, in the same way, the light in human life comes from meditation. (MM 7.2)

Explanation: The bird plays a big role in making the morning beautiful. Similarly, if people want to bring light

Investing can't make you a rich man. You can use that money only in adverse circumstances. If you want to become a rich man then you have to create many sources of income. (MM 7.3)

Explanation: It is seen in society that some people want to keep their money in the bank, so that they can get normal interest on it, but perhaps they do not know that such investment helps them in their opposite situation. If you want to achieve something in your future then you have to do something different and you have to create one or two sources of income.

*****

There will be many hurdles during the journey but you don't need to worry about it, always look ahead and leave everything behind and never look back. (MM 7.4)

Just like a swamp draws you in, too much debt will never allow you to grow in the future. (MM 7.5)

Explanation: As we know that swamp is a kind of hell for any living being as it draws itself. Similarly, too much debt will never let you grow in the future. Therefore, avoid all those dangerous routes where you feel too much risk.

*****

Shadow and bank loans never leave you, It follows you till the last journey. (MM 7.6)

Explanation: shadow and bank both are complement each other. It is seen that people take a lot of loans from banks and sometimes they are unable to repay the loan, I mean to say,

You can save yourself by falling from a bicycle, but you can never save yourself by falling from a motorcycle. So don't forget to wear a helmet. (MM 7.7)

Explanation: in society, many insensible never follow the rule, I think they are full of arrogant. they ride the motorcycle without a helmet and someone rides the car without a seatbelt, as a result, they get an injury during a road accident, always think that your parents, brother, children, and wife are waiting for u. so always wear safety gear during the ride.

*****

Private and govt jobs can terminate you but the business never terminates you. (MM 7.8)

Explanation: You must have seen that during covid-19 many companies fired their servants without any notice.

When someone's heart hurts, the tears never stop. (MM 7.9).

Explanation: In this world, you will find many people who want to hurt you in many ways. But you should never lower your morale because tears make you strong.

*****

Three things are recognized in adversity. Wife in husband's poverty, brother in brother's calamity and children in old age of parents. (MM 7.10)

Explanation: There are many ups and downs in society, but people are recognized only in times of adversity in society. In the same sequence, you can identify three things in your opposite situation. As I mentioned in my quote

Your heart will never be disappointed by donating to the poor, because you know it satisfies you. (MM 7.11)

Explanation: In my view, satisfaction is the best medicine to get relief from expectations etc. If you donate meaningful things to poor people, they will bless you with an open heart and your heart will give you confidence.

*****

Silence can solve your problems, as it is a good alternative to compromise. (MM 7.12)

Expectation: Sometimes people forget in a dispute that one side should remain calm because peace is the only thing where disputes can be avoided.

Only a soldier can fight till his last breath, and remaining is a show-off. (MM 7.13)

Explanation: There should be high respect for the soldiers in this country, as they play an important role in keeping the country safe from enemies etc. Only a soldier can fight till his last breath as he takes an oath to protect his country from any kind of hostile elements. The rest have become victims of confusion.

*****

Never be afraid to fall in business, because one day it will take you to the extreme. (MM 7.14)

Explanation: Some people are always afraid to step into trading because they are afraid of losing money in the market. But without risk, you cannot become a successful

Listening to someone makes you a best friend, and helping someone brings great hope to a relationship. (MM 7.15)

Explanation: Both words play a meaningful role in a relationship or friendship, listening to others makes you his friend because the other should feel that he is listening carefully to his words, in the same way, helping someone has a lot of confidence in friendship.

*****

Excess showing of money is always dangerous, because it is an easy invitation to robbery. (MM 7.16)

Explanation: Some people show their status to people, and some do not show their wealth. The person who never shows

Waste of food can fill the stomach of hungry people, similarly, wastage of water can wet the throat of thirsty people. (MM 7.17)

Explanation: 18% of India's population sleeps without food every day, and some foolish people always throw food in the dustbin. They never think that what I am throwing, can satisfy their hunger. Similarly wasting water is a waste of time. So never waste it because one day you will suffer from it. So always give importance to things.

*****

The poor have no rich friends, similarly, the illiterate have no desire to become rich. (MM 7.18)

Explanation: Always be friends with your counterpart because if poor people befriend rich people, it will not be equal. As you know, poor people will be targeted by rich

Quarrel brings unrest in the house and removes unity so always avoid such quarrels and bring peace among the members, try to solve any problem with a discussion at the dining table. (MM 7.19)

Explanation: There is some problem in every house and there is always some reason behind that dispute, whether it is about money or any other reason. There are always fights and fights about these things, but by compromise, we can avoid quarrels. That's why in my opinion, one should always keep quiet during family quarrels and if possible get away from there for some time, and always try to solve any problem at the dinner table because that is where everyone gathers. and talk about the issues. it's useful, try it.

*****

A girl from another house will rarely be able to take care of your family, As she leaves her home and comes to your home. (MM 7.20)

It is easy to get into offence and dispute by being misled by someone, But it is very difficult to get out of this disease. (MM 7.21)

Explanation: Some people will provoke you to do wrong things because such people always get happy from doing these acts, But at that time, you need to have patience and do your work with good sensibility. If you won't avoid it, you can't come out of this disease, and it will upset you sometimes. You will be confused and unable to take suitable decisions. Therefore, never come under the influence of someone.

*****

Overdoing sometimes causes damage, so always avoid doing so. (MM 7.22)

Explanation: Many times people work more than their

"People can improve themselves by becoming honest, bad politics damages our brotherhood and diversification breaks our Unity."

Seriousness is probably a virtue, but too much seriousness always damages the brain, you need to be focused, not serious. (MM 8.1)

Explanation: You can be serious about many things but not too much, otherwise, you may forget what you have in mind. I saw in the society that some students get serious in their studies which should not happen. You should just focus on everything. By being focused, you will be able to remember everything.

*****

Exploitation has become a magnetic thing against mankind, it is very difficult to remove and it is spreading its feet among us. (MM 8.2)

Explanation: Exploitation has spread among us, and it is

Investment should be on the stock market or SIP, Because by doing this you can become a rich man in future. (MM 8.3)

Explanation: In India, only 5% of the people invest in the stock market etc. because they are afraid that their money might get sunk. but it's not like that. Investment should be in good stocks. Do not invest in penny stocks. If you invest in good stocks, you will make huge profits from them. People should think of setting up income in at least 4 ways because you will get a lot of benefits from this type of scheme.

*****

Know the concept of the subject before arguments, otherwise, there will be no benefit after that. (MM 8.4)

Explanation: I have seen many such people in society who

Too much spicy food damages the organs of the body. Similarly, drinking water with food causes acidity. (MM 8.5)

Explanation: People in India consume a lot of spicy food, which is very risky for the body. Less spicy food is always good for the body and organs but ignorant people depend on refined oils and spices. Smart people don't believe in it. Similarly, drinking water with food causes constipation, so drink water after one hour.

*****

No one knows the pain of heart, only mother and father can understand your feelings. (MM 8.6)

Explanation: There are many people who give you a lot of pain in many ways and there are few people who can

Power is to serve, not to misuse. (MM 8.7)

Explanation: It is seen in society that some responsible persons misuse their powers and are engaged in harming the people with their powers which should not be there. Powers are always there for humanity and powers play an important role in maintaining its beauty always.

*****

Everyone can bother the poor, but very difficult to bother the rich. (MM 8.8)

Explanation: It is an easy target to harass poor people, and everyone can exploit them because they do not have good knowledge. I have seen in society that they are being targeted everywhere but rich people are not because they have an

Modernization reflects the development of the country, in the same way, the standard of living and family education reflects the development of the family. (MM 8.9)

Explanation: I would like to mention here that modernization reflects the development of the government, in the same way, the standard of living reflects the education of the family.

*****

Love is a kind of deception that you need a lot of courage to express yourself, if you are free then avoid it. (MM 8.10)

Explanation: In love, you have to check yourself because many people love others for their lust or something else.

A courageous person never gives up, he always tries to be successful, those who gives-up can never become successful people. (MM 8.11)

Explanation: As I have said always in my previous explanation, if you want to be a successful person then you have to take the risk otherwise you will keep thinking.

*****

You can encourage someone to commit a crime, but you can't get him back on his track. (MM 8.12)

Explanation: Many people in one form or the other incite some people to commit crimes, I think such person is being chosen for the benefit of others. That's why I have always asked to connect with sensible people so that you do not fall into the

Money makes a difference in relationships, and deceit brings a lot of distance to friendship. (MM 8.13)

Explanation: Money indeed draws a very big line in our lives. You must have seen that if someone is not able to return your money in relation then it causes dispute in relationship and friendship. So think before giving money to anyone.

*****

Risk teaches us a lot in life, because it is a good tool to become a successful person. (MM 8.14)

Explanation: As you know, risk has many successful stories, those who took the risk, took the lead, and those who never took the risk were, they are always behind the group. So never be afraid to take a risk.

A leader should be courageous because the condition of the country depends on him, Similarly, the captain of the ship must have complete knowledge, as a failure of command can ruin the future and life. (MM 8.15)

Explanation: Two things can move your country forward: a courageous army and good governance. If they are weak then anyone can capture your country. So choose good governance so that you can feel safe. Similarly, the captain of the ship should be full of wisdom because the failure of command will bring you down.

*****

Just as the index is very important to explain your content, similarly, future planning is important for every family. (MM 8.16)

A cowardly army will never let you feel safe because weapons don't matter, courage should be important. (MM 8.17)

Explanation: A Coward army will never be able to save you from enemies, Technical weapons don't matter. To win any war, courage plays an important role during that time and the presence of mind also matters in the war.

*****

Dream never leaves its effect, it can be good or bad in itself. (MM 8.18)

Explanation: Although, every dream has its own meaning, but according to astrology, if you dream early in the morning, then it will be absolutely true.

*****

Never miss the opportunity, Maybe this will take you further. (MM 8.19)

Explanation: As we know that opportunity brings new hope in our destiny. If we think that by doing something like this we can shape our future then we should do that work, if we miss the opportunity then we will face lot of difficulties in choosing the target. So try to give importance to the opportunity.

*****

Wise people keep quiet and troublemakers create disturbance, and are troubled in themselves. (MM 8.20)

Explanation: A wise person never jumps into an argument before knowing the facts and they are always silent. Such people always use their minds instead of making noise because they know that silence solves everything and fools always create

Star gives us the right direction. In the same way, right path and right advice change our destiny. (MM 8.21)

Explanation: In the olden days, we used to make any strategy against the enemies with the help of stars etc. When we didn't have any kind of technology. But these days we have a lot of sources, so we can plan better. Similarly, someone will provoke you to go against the policies of society and the government, but you should never trust such people because the right decision and the right advice will change your future. So be careful before such an accident. Stay away from negative people and support positive people.

*****

Corruption is a big termite for mankind, which is eating society day by day and it will take us to a big abyss. (MM 8.22)

Explanation: Corruption is spread in society because

Sometimes we write about society, and sometimes we think about society. We want to see society very closely because many selfish people in the queue will never let you grow. (MM 8.23)

Explanation: As I have mentioned in many of my interpretations, society is selfish. There are almost people who see their advantage. Although some people support the truth. For example, if you develop yourself in your goal, many people will pull your leg. That's why I say society is selfish.

*****

A cheater never corrects himself, because he has never been with good people. (MM 8.24)

Explanation: There is no dearth of fraudsters in society

No one can understand your feelings because responsible people only know their generation, you will keep on crying and no one will help you, you have to survive by your courage. (MM 8.25)

Explanation: I am indicating to those people who never care about poor people or middle-class families. They want to build their children's future and earn more money. They consume the government budget and use it for their new work. But they never do anything for the poor people and the country. If you want to do something, you have to live by your guts.

*****

Never hide your ability because if you do this then you will never be able to become a successful person, always try to find your new path. (MM 8.26)

Every morning we think about new work, but few people get the chance to fulfil the dream. (MM 8.27)

Explanation: It is said that karma is predominant, so a person should start his daily routine with good deeds and worship so that his whole day is happy, but only a few people get karma because karma follows him.

*****

Diversification breaks the unity of the family, and where there is union the home is happy. (MM 8.28)

Explanation: There is a lot of power in unity in itself. No one can break it. But if you argue with each other then it will be easy for those who are targeting your family. Hence unity

Connecting with devotion is as important for a human being as ink for a pen. (MM 8.29)

Explanation: Worship and meditation are the only sources of salvation. People are forgetting their duty by not worshipping. Hence they remain confused with their mind and unable to concentrate on their work, hence worship is necessary for human beings.

*****

Epilogue

Never be a slave because a job only enslaves you, doesn't give freedom, you have to find a good way to freedom. (EP. 1.1)

*****

In society, you will find people who will exploit you and look at you with bad eyes, Always beware of such men.   (EP 1.2)

*****

It is important to respect elders in your life.

All things matter and all things must be examined and tested. (EP 1.3)

Notes.

Most of the following confessions/quotes under numbers are themselves explaining the reality of life and society which is happening in real life and here I have tried to express my views for the society as we know that people in books Have good thoughts for the society. But the reality on the ground is different. You have to read all the quotes carefully to know better.

About Author

I am Manmohan Shukla who belongs to district Fatehpur (UP). It is 100 km away from Prayagraj. As you know, Prayagraj is a place where a lot of devotees from all over the world come to take a holy dip in the Sangam River. You can also visit Ayodhya which is the birthplace of Lord Shri Ram. It is 110 km away from Prayagraj. I took my education from Kendriya Vidyalaya, Prayagraj and for some reason, I left my graduation in the middle,

I joined the CAPF in 2010, and since that time I have contributed to several places like insurgency, red corridor and Kisan Movement etc. which happened in 2021. But I have always aspired to do something different, that's why I choose this way to spread my views across the world, so that people can know real things, This book will help you to understand, what is happening in society. This is my first